Copyright © 2015, 2019 by Vivian Sihshu Yenika.

ISBN   Softcover   978-1-951469-81-8

All rights reserved. No part of this book may be reproduced or transmitted in any form or by any means, electronic or mechanical, including photocopying, recording, or by any information storage and retrieval system without express written permission from the author, except in the case of brief quotations embodied in critical reviews and certain other non-commercial uses permitted by copyright law.

This novel is a work of fiction. Names, descriptions, entities, and incidents included in the story are products of the author's imagination. Any resemblance to actual persons, events, and entities is entirely coincidental.

Printed in the United States of America.

To order additional copies of this book, contact:
Bookwhip
1-855-339-3589
https://www.bookwhip.com

For Durell Timah

My name is Berdu, and I live at an oil palm plantation in Cameroon. One day at school, Bayena, Boti, and Bate sat on the verandah, bragging about their fathers.

"My dad is a manager," Bayena said.

"Supervisor," Boti beamed.

"King of the road!" Bate leaped off his seat, clapping his chest. *Clap! Clap! Clap!*

"King of the road?"

"Yes! He builds roads!"

"Cool!"

Then they looked at me.

Those rich kids!

At home I asked what Papa did. But Papa simply dropped his lunch bag on the floor and aired his work overalls.

Then Mama said, "Papa needs his supper."

So I waited.

Mama brought him *garri* and *okro* soup. The steam rose high to the ceiling. I caught some with my bare hands, but it melted away. I tried again.

And again. And then I gave up.

Papa was gobbling balls of garri.

When Papa finished, he hooked my head in his elbow and ruffled my hair. "What are you up to, son?"

"P-papa," I stuttered.

"Yes, my child."

"Nothing."

He let go.

Later, he snatched a bucket, wrapped a towel around his neck, and walked toward the public bathroom. I trailed behind. We passed brick houses and tall palm trees.

One-room…two-room…palm tree.

Small, big…small, big.

And each time someone waved at Papa.

"*How na*, Patrick?" the fathers saluted.

"*How na*, Mr. Bongfen?" the mothers greeted.

"Good evening, Papa Berdu," the children shouted.

Papa nodded. "Fine. How are you too? Thank *wuna*, my children."

At last we arrived at the bathroom stalls. The line was not long. Papa filled his bucket and entered one stall. I waited by the laundry platform.

And waited…

Then Papa came out with an empty bucket and his towel on one shoulder.

"Hold this." He leaned forward and rubbed some lotion.

It smelled good! I sniffed the air then reached for the lotion bottle. Papa seized it and tickled my belly. I laughed hard. Papa laughed too.

At night, Papa told Mama he was going to the employee's club. I followed and peeked. First, he played ping-pong. The ball flew *vroom* and landed *pong*. *Vroom* and *pong*…*vroom* and *pong*. He won the match. That was my papa!

He spotted me and came over with a stick of peppery *suya*. My eyes lit up; then I ran behind the building and ate it all by myself. It was a great night!

The next day, when Papa got up to go to work, I tiptoed after him all the way to where the *gwongworo* stood waiting for him and the others.

"Workers," the driver shouted, "harvesting is at Field 16."

"Okay, Oga," Papa and his friends answered.

That field was quite close to my school.

Papa chucked his work tools in the truck. Next went his lunch bag then him.

As the gwongworo pulled out, they sang, "Oh ho. Oh ho. Ho! Ho! Oh ho. Ho! Ho! Ho! Ho!"

Standing in the shadows, I echoed until their voices grew fainter and fainter until it ceased.

Classes dragged at school that day. Mr. Oto said all my sums were wrong, my letters were crooked…my *everything* was wrong!

"Son, what is the matter with you today?"

The bell rang.

Mr. Oto placed a hand over his forehead. "Go then, Berdu,"

I ran nonstop to Field 16.

And there was Papa next to a palm tree, harvesting bunches of ripe palm fruits. First, he hooked the large bunch with his Malayan knife and shook it one, two, three, four, five times. Then he released and stepped aside. The massive bunch came tumbling.

"Wow!"

Papa hooked another, and another, and another. One, two, three, four! There! A bunch landed with a loud thud, shaking the ground.

Papa smiled and placed the fruits in two separate baskets attached to a long bamboo. He balanced the bamboo across his shoulders and headed to the drop-off site. As he approached, I watched from behind some shrubs. He jogged right past me, panting. *Hem! Hem! Hem!* The ground shook after him.

"Papa," I whispered.

When Papa returned, he gathered his tools and waded across a stream to the next row.

"Wait up, Papa," I called.

He scratched his head. "Berdu?"

"Uh, hu."

"You could get hurt."

Sweat glided down his face.

"Here, have some, Papa." I offered him water in a leafy cup I made.

"*Weh*, my child."

He drank the water. *Gong, gong, gong.*

"Thanks, son. Run along now." He ruffled my hair.

"But, Papa…!"

"Yes?" Eyes lighting up he said, "I cut palm fruits! I am cutting *mbanga*!"

At school I announced that Papa had a cool job too.

"Yes, Bayena," I bragged. "He cuts palm fruits!"

"That's not a job!" Bate giggled.

"But, of course," Mr. Oto chimed.

"Huh?"

"I told you!"

That evening when Papa came home, I rushed to *elay* him. He opened his arms wide and engulfed me. He flung me side to side then up and down, laughing loud. I laughed loud too. Tears rolled down our faces.

Glossary of Words

Camp – as described in this story, it is a series of small one-or two-room brick houses used by different families

Elay – to hug

Wuna – collective pronoun for "you"

Gwongworo – truck

Malayan knife – sickle attached on a long bamboo pole used to harvest bunches of palm fruits from the stalks of tall palm trees

Oga – boss

Okro soup – sauce made with okra

Suya – beef Shish kebab

Lobe is pronounced "Law beh"

www.ingramcontent.com/pod-product-compliance
Lightning Source LLC
Chambersburg PA
CBHW040201100526
44591CB00006B/60